The Main Ingredient

presents:

Mildred Smith's
Traditional Recipes

in association with

GRANADA
TELEVISION

Published by Sigma Leisure - an imprint of
Sigma Press, 1 South Oak Lane, Wilmslow, Cheshire SK9 6AR, England.

British Library Cataloguing in Publication Data
A CIP record for this book is available from the British Library.

ISBN: 1-85058-480-X

Editorial, typesetting and page design by: Sigma Press, Wilmslow, Cheshire.

Cover design: Lynne Abbott, Manchester Free Press.
Cover photographs: Mildred Smith (main picture) and *The Main Ingredient* presenter, Lucy Meacock and reporter, Mark Owen (Granada Television Ltd)

Illustrations: Martin Mills

Production Team for *The Main Ingredient*:
Researchers: Vicky Matthews, Charlotte Hindle, Jason Collier
Production Secretary: Mandy O'Toole
Cameras: Gordon MacGregor, Dougie Hallows
Sound Recordists: David Hollingworth, Tony Cooper
Electricians: Terry Mottershead, Tommy Kershaw
Executive Producer: Mike Spencer
Director: Tim Hopewell
Producer: Debbie Pollitt

Acknowledgments
With thanks to Barbara Densem BSc MSc, and her students at The Department of Food and Consumer Technology, Hollings Faculty, Manchester Metropolitan University.

Printed by: Manchester Free Press

I've always enjoyed cooking . . .

...not surprising really, as I do come from a long line of good cooks. The women in my family have always believed that the way to a man's heart is through his stomach – most young women today won't go along with such an old-fashioned idea, I'm sure, but I believe that our culinary skills are the ones most appreciated by our families.

Cooking for people is a way of showing your love for them – that has always been my motivation, my mother's before me, and her mother before her.

Imagine my delight now, so unexpectedly late in life, at having the opportunity to share some cooking secrets with you, and recipes which my family has grown up with. There's a lot to be said for traditional dishes and I'm glad to find that more and more people are rediscovering this sort of cookery.

I've had a lovely time being part of The Main Ingredient and working with Granada Television – I hope you get as much pleasure from the recipes in this book.

Good luck, good cooking – and happy eating!

Mildred Smith

Contents

Healthy Eating Note!

Mildred Smith uses traditional ingredients in these recipes. In most cases, lard and butter can be substituted by mono- or polyunsaturated margarines. Where frying is involved, vegetable oil can be used. These changes will reduce the intake of saturated fats in line with current dietary opinion.

Soups, Main Courses & Accompaniments

Except where indicated, main course recipes are for four people.

Leek and Potato Soup

"There's nothing like the wonderful smell of Leek and Potato Soup – it takes me right back to when I was a girl. Mum would always have a pot on the go for when Dad came in off the late shift. With a chunk of crusty bread, it's a wholesome winter warmer."

Ingredients

2 lbs (900g) leeks

2 lbs (900g) potatoes, peeled and thickly sliced

2 oz (50g) butter

3 pints (1.8 litres) stock or water and stock cubes (chicken or vegetable)

¼ pint (150ml) creamy milk

¼ pint (150ml) single cream

chopped chives – optional

Method

Trim and wash the leeks thoroughly, then slice them into 1" (2cm) chunks. Heat the fat in a large pan, add the leeks and cook for 5 minutes, add the potatoes and stock, cover the pan and cook for half an hour, then liquidise.

Return the soup to the pan, add the milk and reheat. Season to taste with salt and pepper. Stir a spoonful of cream into each bowl and sprinkle with chives. Serve with crusty bread.

Haddock Chowder

"When I was a girl, Tuesday was always fish night in our house and I loved it when mum made a thick and warming Haddock Chowder – a very comforting dish to eat."

Ingredients

2 medium onions, peeled and coarsely chopped

2 large potatoes, peeled and diced

¾ pint (425ml) water

3 rashers of bacon cut into strips

1½ lbs (700g) smoked haddock

¾ pint (425ml) milk

8 fl oz (275ml) double cream

salt and pepper to taste

Method

Bring the onions, potatoes and water to the boil, and cook over a moderate heat for 10 minutes. Fry the bacon until crisp.

Add the onion, potatoes and liquid to the bacon and fat. Add the haddock and milk, cover and simmer for 10 – 15 minutes, until the fish is tender enough to flake. Add the cream, heat through and season to taste. Eat with crusty brown bread and butter.

Toad in the Hole

"A great one for the kids – a friend of mine says that her little boy's convinced there are real toads in there! And who is she to spoil his fun? Go on, give 'em a tasty tease!"

Ingredients

4 oz (110g) plain flour

a pinch of salt and pepper

1 large egg

¼ pint (150ml) milk

¼ pint (150ml) water

1 lb (450g) of pork sausages

Method

Sift the flour, salt and pepper into a mixing bowl. Break the egg into it, and using a wooden spoon, work in the flour from the sides. Beat in half the milk and water, beat for a minute, then add the rest and beat to a smooth batter.

Heat the oven to Gas Mark 7 or 220°C, lay the sausages in a greased dish and bake for 10 minutes. Remove the dish from the oven, stand it on a baking tray, and pour in the batter. Cook for 30 – 35 minutes, until the batter is well-risen and sausages are golden brown.

Chicken and Leek Cobbler

"When my mother taught me to cook she said, 'Mildred, make variety the spice of your life.' So I did, and a nice change for chicken is this leek and chicken cobbler – it's one of my favourites."

Ingredients

1 lb (450g) chicken (preferably breast) chopped into bite size
    pieces
2 tablespoons (30ml) seasoned flour
2 tablespoons (30ml) cooking oil
8 oz (225g) leeks, cleaned and sliced
4 fl oz (125ml) chicken stock
7 fl oz (200ml) milk

Method

Toss the chicken in the seasoned flour. Heat the oil in a large frying pan. Add the chicken and leeks and fry gently for about 15 minutes, until sealed on all sides. Add the stock and milk, cover and simmer for 10 minutes. Pour into a shallow, greased, oven-proof dish and cook at Gas Mark 4 or 180°C for 15 minutes. Then top with Cheese Scones as follows:

Cheese Scones

Ingredients

8 oz (225g) self-raising flour
a pinch of salt and pepper
1 oz (25g) margarine
3 oz (75g) grated cheese
$\frac{1}{2}$ teaspoon (2.5ml) English mustard powder
1 egg, size 3
4 tablespoons (60ml) milk

Method

Mix seasonings and mustard into flour, rub in fat, add cheese and mix to a soft dough with egg and milk. Cut into rounds $\frac{1}{2}$" (1cm) thick and arrange on top of the cooked chicken mixture. Sprinkle on a little more cheese and bake for about 10 minutes or until well-risen, at Gas Mark 6 or 200°C.

Pork and Sage Pudding with Apple Sauce

"My husband used to say I'd have muscles bigger than his with all the chopping of apples for this meal. But it was worth it when he tasted my Pork and Sage Pudding. He loved it!"

Ingredients

1 lb (450g) minced pork or pork sausage meat

1 large onion, peeled and finely chopped

4 oz (110g) white breadcrumbs

2 teaspoons (10ml) dried sage

1 large egg

salt and pepper

½ lb (225g) cooking apples

sugar to taste

a squeeze of lemon juice

Method

Mix all the main ingredients together, seasoning to taste. Grease a 2 pint (1.2 litre) basin and sprinkle a little brown sugar round the sides. Add the pork mixture, cover and then cook at Gas Mark 4 or 180°C for about 30 minutes.

Turn out and serve in slices with apple sauce.

To Make The Sauce: peel and slice the apples, cover with water and cook till tender. Add a squeeze of lemon and sugar as liked.

Alternatively, this dish can be cooked in a microwave. Place ingredients in a basin and cover with greaseproof paper. Put basin in another dish containing enough cold water to come half way up the sides of the basin.

Microwave on high for 25 minutes (650watt), remove paper cover after 15 minutes. Adjust time as necessary, in proportion to power.

Stilton Flan

"I'm always being asked, 'Mildred, how can I make cheese more interesting?' I always say, 'Why not make a Stilton flan?' It's a great choice for cheese!"

Ingredients

8 oz (225g) shortcrust pastry (see 'pastry' section in this book) to line the tin.

Filling

1½ oz (40g) butter

1½ oz (40g) plain flour

¼ pint (150ml) milk

8 fl oz (275ml) single cream

4 oz (110g) Stilton cheese, crumbled

8 oz (225g) cottage cheese

3 eggs, size 3

about 4 tablespoons (60ml) chopped chives

salt and pepper to season

Method

Line a greased 9" (23cm) flan tin with the pastry. Melt the butter in a saucepan. Take off the heat and stir in the flour.

Add the milk and cream, bring the sauce to the boil, stirring briskly, take off heat and beat in the two cheeses, the beaten eggs and chopped chives. Season to taste.

Pour the mixture carefully into the lined tin. Lift onto a pre-heated baking sheet and bake above the centre of the oven on Gas Mark 6 or 200°C for 10 minutes then turn down to Gas Mark 4 or 180°C for 40 minutes. Check that the filling is firmly set.

Beef Stew with Dumplings

"Here's a dish that goes way back – and what a great way to warm 'em up in winter. It may not be exotic but I'm sure there's not many who'd turn down such a nourishing meal. Go on, dish out the dumplings!"

Ingredients

1½ – 2 lbs (700g – 900g) lean stewing beef
2 lamb kidneys (halved and cored)
8 oz (225g) onions, peeled and quartered
8 oz (225g) carrots, peeled and sliced
1 oz (25g) seasoned flour
1 oz (25g) lard or dripping
¼ level teaspoon (1.25ml) of grated nutmeg
1½ pints (845ml) beef stock (or, if not available, the same volume of water and a stock cube)

Dumplings

4 oz (110g) self-raising flour
2 oz (50g) suet
2 oz (50g) finely chopped onion
1 level teaspoon (5ml) mixed herbs
a good pinch of salt
cold water to mix

Method

Trim excess fat from the meat, and cut into neat pieces. Toss the meat and kidney in the seasoned flour, reserving about 1 tablespoon (15ml) of flour. Heat the fat in a frying-pan, add the meat, cook until brown on all sides, then remove and put into a large saucepan.

Add the onions and carrots to the meat. If necessary, add a little more fat to the frying-pan, add the reserved flour and cook until it starts to brown. (This gives colour and thickness).

Stir in the stock gradually and bring to the boil, season with salt and pepper to taste, also adding the nutmeg. Pour over the meat and vegetables, scraping all the bits from the pan. Cover and simmer for 1½ – 2 hours until the meat is tender.

30 minutes before the end of cooking time, make the dumplings. Stir in the flour and salt together, then add the herbs, suet and onions. Stir well. Mix to a soft, but not sticky, dough as you add cold water. With floured hands, divide into 10 pieces and roll into balls. Coat lightly with flour and place on top of the stew. Cover with a lid and cook for 30 minutes.

This dish may be cooked in the oven, centre shelf, Gas Mark 3 or 170°C for 2 – 2½ hours. Dumplings take 35 minutes to cook in the oven.

Cornish Pasties

"I love going for long walks in the country and instead of sandwiches in my packed lunch, I take Cornish Pasties – a much tastier option!"

Ingredients

8 oz (225g) self-raising flour
4 oz (110g) hard fat or dripping
a pinch of salt
cold water to mix

Filling

2 heaped tablespoons (30ml) potatoes, peeled and diced
8 oz (225g) stewing steak, fat removed and cut into very small
  pieces
1 small onion, peeled and chopped
salt and pepper

Method

Rub the fat into the flour and salt, mix to a soft dough and roll out to about ¼" (1cm) thick on a floured board. Cut into 6" (15cm) circles.

Combine the filling ingredients and moisten with 3 – 4 tablespoons (45ml – 60ml) stock or water.

Put a small amount of filling into each pastry circle, damp the edges, and fold into half, pressing the edges together and fluting with the thumb and finger.

Stand on a greased baking tray with the fluted edges pointing upwards.

Brush with milk and bake at Gas Mark 7 or 220°C for about 10 minutes. The turn the heat down to Gas Mark 4, 350°F or 180°C and bake for a further 50 minutes.

Old English Casserole

"If I'm entertaining friends or family, I often make this casserole – it's a favourite with everyone and once it's done, it's done, so you can enjoy the evening!"

Ingredients

1 large oxtail cut into joints

8 oz (225g) butter beans

2 onions, peeled and chopped

2 carrots, peeled and sliced

1 oz (25g) flour

1 oz (25g) butter

a pinch of marjoram (or mixed herbs)

¾ pint (425ml) of stock or water and cube

2 teaspoons (10ml) lemon juice

salt and pepper

Method

Soak the beans overnight in cold water. Pre-heat the oven to Gas Mark 5 or 190°C. Melt the butter in a frying-pan and fry the oxtail until golden, then transfer to greased casserole. Fry the onions and add to the meat.

Sprinkle the flour into the pan, stir and add the stock gradually, stirring well. Pour over the meat, add the butter beans, (well-drained) the carrot, herbs and lemon juice. Season with salt and pepper. Cover with lid or foil and cook in the centre of the oven for 30 minutes. Reduce the heat to Gas Mark 2 or 150°C and cook for 2½ – 3 hours until the meat is tender.

Notes: Canned butter beans may be substituted, in which case add to the casserole about 30 minutes before end of cooking time. After the frying stage, the mixture could be transferred to a slow cooker, high for about half an hour, then turned on low for all day if necessary.

Creamed Tripe and Onions

"Tripe's always been the butt of jokes, hasn't it? Well laugh away, I say – it's on all the top chefs' menus these days!"

Ingredients

1½ lb (700g) tripe (ox or thick seam)

1 large onion, diced

1 large carrot, diced

2 bay leaves

1 teaspoon (5ml) salt

¾ pint (425ml) milk

1 oz (25g) butter or margarine

1 oz (25g) flour

2 slices bread (for croutons)

oil or lard for frying

Method

Wash tripe thoroughly, drain, dry and cut into 3" (8cm) squares. Put in a pan with carrot, onion, bay leaves and ½ pint (275ml) milk. Bring almost to the boil, then turn down and simmer until tripe is tender (about 1½ hours). Melt the margarine in a pan, stir in flour and add remaining ¼ pint (150ml) of milk – stirring well. Add tripe, onion, and other ingredients to the sauce and season to taste. Serve in a warmed dish with croutons.

To make your own croutons: cut bread (crusts removed) into 8 triangles and fry in oil or lard until golden. Serve on dish.

Leeks and Ham

"If the man in your life is a Welshman, feed him a bit of his national culinary heritage – go on, get out the leeks!"

Ingredients

8 slices boiled ham

8 medium-sized leeks

1 pint (600ml) of milk

2 oz (50g) flour

2 oz (50g) margarine

4 oz (110g) full flavoured cheese (ie Cheddar)

1 tablespoon (15ml) breadcrumbs and some grated cheese

Method

Wash and trim the leeks. Drop into boiling salted water and cook for 10 minutes. Drain and wrap each leek in a slice of ham. Put into a shallow, greased baking dish. Melt the margarine, add flour, then milk, stirring to make a smooth sauce. Add cheese and season to taste. Pour over leeks, sprinkle with breadcrumbs and extra cheese and cook for about 20 minutes at Gas Mark 4 or 180°C. If preferred, brown under a hot grill. Eat with crusty brown bread and butter.

Rabbit and Cabbage Casserole

"Rabbit was often on the menu when mum was cooking – no-one asked where it came from in those days but sure enough, as if by magic, every fortnight a rabbit would appear in the kitchen. Strange – but delicious."

Ingredients

1 oz (25g) lard

2 rashers streaky bacon, de-rinded and chopped

1 large onion, peeled and sliced

½ lb (225g) cooking apples, peeled, cored and sliced

1½ lbs (700g) white cabbage, washed and coarsely shredded

1 lb (450g) boneless rabbit, cut into chunks

2 oz (50g) plain flour

2 level teaspoons (10ml) English mustard powder

½ teaspoon (2.5ml) salt and pepper

½ pint (275ml) cider and ½ pint (275ml) water or

1 pint (570ml) of stock (chicken or vegetable)

Method

Melt lard in frying pan, add onion and bacon and cook until onion is soft. Add apple slices and cook for 2 minutes. Place onion mixture and cabbage in a casserole dish in alternate layers, finishing with cabbage.

Toss rabbit in flour, mustard and seasonings until evenly coated. Place on top of cabbage. Pour over stock, Cover and cook for about 2 hours at Gas Mark 4 or 180°C until the cabbage is soft and the rabbit is tender.

Kedgeree

"In the days of the Raj, Kedgeree was King – here's my version of a classic colonial dish."

Ingredients

1 lb (450g) smoked haddock

1 medium-sized onion, peeled and chopped

8 oz (225g) long grain rice

1 teaspoon (5ml) curry powder

1½ pints (875ml) water

6 fl oz (200ml) milk

3 hard-boiled eggs, 2 chopped and 1 sliced

salt and black pepper

1½ oz (40g) butter

1 tablespoon (15ml) chopped parsley

Method

Heat the oil in a large saucepan and fry onion until soft. Stir in curry powder, add rice, mixing well. Pour in water and simmer for about 15 minutes until rice absorbs water and is tender. If necessary, add a little more boiling water. Put the haddock and milk in a large frying pan over moderate heat. Bring to boil and simmer for 2 minutes. Break the fish into large flakes. Add to rice with butter, chopped egg and seasonings. Garnish with sliced egg and parsley.

Shepherd's Pie

"Picture the scene . . . it's a wet and windy winter's afternoon. But the house is warm and cosy, and the reassuring aroma of Shepherd's Pie is drifting out from the kitchen – it almost makes winter worthwhile, doesn't it?"

Ingredients

1 lb (450g) minced meat (lamb, beef or pork)

1 large onion

1 tablespoon (15ml) tomato puree (or 2 tomatoes peeled and chopped)

½ pint (275ml) of stock

1 oz (25g) cornflour

1½ lbs (700g) potatoes, peeled

salt and pepper

green and red pepper (optional)

Method

Boil the potatoes. Drain and mash with milk and butter. Chop onion finely and fry in a little oil until soft. Add the meat and brown. Finely grate a carrot and add to the meat. Fry both for another 5 minutes. If you like, add a little chopped green and red pepper. Add stock and bring to the boil. Thicken with cornflour, add tomato puree and put into a greased dish.

Pipe the mashed potato over the top and sprinkle with grated Cheddar cheese.

Pre-heat the oven to Gas Mark 4 or 180°C and bake for about 30 minutes.

Lancashire Hot-Pot

"I believe that Northern food is the best -- especially when it's a hot and steaming Lancashire hot-pot. Go on, warm yourselves up and make one tonight."

Ingredients

2 lbs (900g) middle neck chops of lamb

12 oz (350g) onions, peeled and sliced

6 oz (175g) mushrooms, sliced

1½ lbs (700g) potatoes, peeled and thickly sliced

1 pint (570ml) of stock

a little butter

salt and pepper

Method

In a greased casserole dish, alternate layers of lamb chops and onions, seasoning each layer. Add the mushrooms and pour in the stock to cover the meat and onions. Finally, add potato in overlapping layers, dotting with small pieces of butter.

Cook in a pre-heated oven at Gas Mark 4 or 180°C for about 2½ hours with dish covered. After 1½ hours remove cover and allow potatoes to brown.

Steak and Kidney Pie with Rough Puff Pastry

"The best culinary double act in the business if you ask me – steak and kidney . . . the pie to savour!"

Ingredients

8 oz rough puff pastry (see 'pastry' section in this book)

Filling

1 lb (450g) rump steak, cut into cubes and tossed in seasoned flour

12 oz (350g) kidney, trimmed and tossed in flour

6 oz (175g) mushrooms, sliced

½ pint (275ml) of stock

1 tablespoon (15ml) cornflour

Method

Layer the steak and kidney into a greased pie-dish. Add the stock, slightly thickened with the cornflour, mix to smooth paste. Cover with foil and cook for 1½ hours at Gas Mark 5 or 190°C, adding more stock if the meat becomes dry. Allow to cool completely before adding mushrooms. This filling may be made the day before you need it.

Roll out the pastry into a circle 1" (2cm) larger than the dish. Cut off 1" (2cm) strip. Brush with cold water and put round the edge of the dish. Place the remaining circle of pastry on top. Seal and brush with milk.

Bake at Gas Mark 7 or 220°C for 10 minutes, then reduce heat to Gas Mark 4 or 180°C and bake for 25 minutes until crisp and golden.

Tip: Here's my tip for the best results . . . As I personally don't like pastry to get damp underneath, I usually cover the filling with foil and lay the pastry on a baking sheet alongside to cook separately."

Cheese and Onion Pie

"Cheese and onion pie, that completely tasty combination, comes to you as one of my own particular favourites. Great for vegetarians too!"

Ingredients

8 oz (225g) shortcrust pastry (see 'pastry' section in this book)

Filling

1½ lbs (700g) onions, peeled and sliced

6oz (175g) mature cheddar cheese, grated

2 large eggs, beaten

½ oz (10g) margarine

1 level teaspoon (5ml) English mustard powder

A good pinch of ground nutmeg

Method

Put onions, margarine and nutmeg into a pan. Cook gently over low heat until soft but not coloured – about 10 minutes. Shake the pan occasionally to prevent sticking. Transfer to a bowl and leave to cool. Roll pastry out. Grease a large pie plate 9" (23cm) – 10" (25cm). Line the plate with half the dough.

Add the grated cheese, mustard and beaten eggs to the onion mixture, mix well and spoon onto pastry base. Roll out the other half, and cover the plate. If you like, cut the pastry into strips and arrange in a lattice pattern. Brush with milk. Bake above the centre of a pre-heated oven for about 30 minutes, or until pastry is golden.

Gas Mark 6 or 200°C.

Pan Haggerty

"I learnt this recipe when I was on holiday in Northumberland as a girl – it's so simple and so tasty you'll love it! And it's an excellent way of using up your potatoes."

Ingredients

1 lb (450g) potatoes, peeled

2 oz (50g) butter or margarine

8 oz (220g) onions, peeled and finely chopped

4 oz (110g) Cheddar cheese, grated

salt and black pepper

Method

Grate the potatoes and put into a colander. Cover with a plate or paper towel and press to remove surplus starch. Melt half the butter in a frying pan, add the onions and fry gently until transparent. Remove from the pan. Add the remaining butter, spread the potatoes evenly, then add the onions.

Season with salt and pepper and sprinkle with the cheese. Cook very gently for about 10 minutes until the bottom browns. Put a plate over the Pan Haggerty and turn onto it.

Melt a little more butter in the pan and slide the mixture carefully back to brown the other side.

Cook for a further 10 minutes until the pancake is cooked right through and browned on both sides. Slide it onto a warmed plate and serve at once.

Mince and Batter Pudding

"The men in my family have always had a preference for puds – and this savoury one certainly goes down a treat in our house. Go on, pass 'em a pud!"

Ingredients
(for 2 people)

4 oz (110g) plain flour

2 eggs, size 2

½ level teaspoon (2.5ml) salt

½ pint (275ml) of milk, or milk and water mixed

½ oz (10g) lard

½ lb (225g) minced beef

1 level teaspoon (5ml) horseradish sauce

pepper and salt

1 beef stock cube

2 shallow oven-proof dishes or small roasting tin

Method

Set the oven to Gas Mark 7 or 220°C. Make a batter, sifting flour and salt into a basin, beating the egg with the milk till smooth.

Place half the fat in each dish and heat in the oven for 3 minutes. Mix the mince, horseradish sauce, salt and pepper and crumbled stock cube.

Divide between the two dishes, return to the oven for 5 minutes. Pour the batter over the meat and cook for 20 minutes, or until well-risen and golden brown. Serve immediately.

Pork and Baked Beans

"If pork's a particular favourite with you, put it together with beans like this and serve it up for a late night supper. What a tasty treat!"

Ingredients

1 lb (450g) lean diced pork, cut into cubes

2 oz (50g) butter

2 rashers of streaky bacon, de-rinded and cut into strips

1 lb (450g) dried haricot beans, soaked overnight in cold water, then par-boiled for 10 minutes (or tinned beans to avoid soaking)

12 oz (350g) tomatoes, peeled

½ teaspoon (2.5ml) salt

½ teaspoon (2.5ml) pepper

¼ teaspoon (1.25ml) dried basil (or mixed herbs)

¼ teaspoon (1.25ml) dried thyme (or mixed herbs)

2 teaspoons (10ml) sugar

1 pint (570ml) of stock (preferably vegetable)

Method

Heat 1½ oz (40g) of butter in a frying pan and fry the cubed pork till lightly brown all over. Grease a deep casserole with the remaining butter and lay the bacon strips at the bottom.

Pass the tomatoes through a sieve, season with salt and pepper and add the herbs and sugar. Add the stock to the puree and mix well.

Drain the par-boiled beans, put half of them into the casserole. Put the pork on top, then add the rest of the beans. Pour the stock over the beans and meat, cover with a lid or foil and cook in the pre-heated oven for about 4 hours at Gas Mark 2 or 150°C.

Note: this dish can be made in a slow cooker, used as a casserole, after the first stages.

Lamb Ragout

"It's maximum flavour with this lovely lamb recipe – a wonderful dish as a summer casserole."

Ingredients

1½ lbs (700g) middle neck lamb chops

2 oz (50g) fat

1 large onion, peeled and chopped

1 large carrot, peeled and grated

2 oz (50g) bacon, chopped

8 oz (225g) can tomatoes, or 3 fresh, skinned and chopped

2 level tablespoons (30ml) tomato puree

2 level tablespoons (30ml) plain flour, seasoned with salt and pepper

½ pint (300ml) stock (not beef) or water

a pinch of mixed spice

Method

Melt half the fat in a large frying pan which has a lid (or use a large saucepan). Add the onion, carrot and bacon and fry gently till lightly coloured. Transfer to a plate.

Trim excess fat from the meat and remove the spinal cord. Toss the meat in the seasoned flour and fry in the remaining fat. Return the onion mixture to the pan, stir in the tomatoes, tomato puree, the stock and spice. Bring to the boil, then reduce the heat, cover with the lid (or foil) and simmer gently for about 1½ hours until the meat is tender. Check for seasoning and serve with new potatoes and green peas.

Herring Pie

"Mealtimes will go swimmingly if you feed them with fish! (But jokes like that may affect the digestion . . . !)"

Ingredients

4 herrings, cleaned, boned and filleted
salted water
1 oz (25g) butter
4 medium potatoes, thinly sliced
2 medium cooking apples, peeled and finely chopped
salt and pepper

Method

Soak the prepared fish in the salted water for 1 hour. Rub the butter over the sides and bottom of a straight-sided pie dish.

Line the sides and bottom with some to the potato slices. Layer the fish and apple, seasoning with salt and pepper and finish with a layer of potato slices.

Cover with a well-buttered paper, bake at Gas Mark 4 or 180°C for 45 minutes.

15 minutes before the end of cooking time remove the paper to brown the top.

Devilled Chicken

"Tantalise your taste-buds with this tasty meal – (forgive the alliteration!). It's a devil of a dish!"

Ingredients

4 chicken portions

2 level tablespoons (30ml) mango chutney or homemade chutney

1 tablespoon (15ml) malt vinegar

1 tablespoon (15ml) Worcester sauce

2 tablespoons (30ml) cooking oil

2 level teaspoons (10ml) English mustard powder

pepper and salt

a pinch of mixed herbs

Method

Set the oven to Gas Mark 6 or 200°C. Lay the chicken portions in a greased shallow oven-proof dish. Put the remaining ingredients into a basin and beat well with a fork.

Pour over the chicken, coating completely. Cook for about 1 hour or until chicken is tender. Baste the chicken with the sauce two or three times during cooking.

Turkey in Coconut Sauce

"If you think you've had your fill of turkey after Christmas or Easter, but you've still got a fridge full of leftovers, here's an exotic solution. Go on, have a spicy treat!"

Ingredients

1¼ lb (450g) turkey breast (cooked) cut into bite-size pieces

1 medium onion, peeled and finely chopped

3 medium carrots, sliced

3 oz (75g) creamed coconut, chopped roughly

1 chicken stock cube

1 can of pineapple rings in juice

¼ pint (150ml) of boiling water

a pinch of cinnamon

black pepper to taste

a knob of butter

1 teaspoon (5ml) cooking oil

Method

Heat the oil in a large frying pan and cook onion over a medium heat until golden. Move to one side, add turkey pieces and brown on all sides. Add the carrots. dissolve the stock cube in boiling water and add the juice from the can of pineapple. Add the turkey and season with pepper and taste.

Bring to the boil, then simmer gently for 15 minutes, stirring occasionally. Add the creamed coconut and stir until melted.

In a separate pan, fry the pineapple rings in the butter, until lightly browned. Serve with the turkey.

Cheese and Bacon Shorties

"My son used to love these shorties when he came in from school – they're fun to eat and they fill 'em up until it's time for dinner."

Ingredients

4 oz (110g) streaky bacon, de-rinded

6 oz (175g) plain flour

4 oz (110g) butter

4 oz (110g) grated Cheddar cheese

½ level teaspoon (2.5ml) English mustard powder

salt and pepper

¼ teaspoon (1.25ml) paprika

Method

Grill the bacon until crisp, cool and cut into small pieces. Sift the flour, salt, mustard and paprika into a bowl and rub in the butter. Mix in the bacon and cheese and work into a soft dough.

Press into a greased tin 11" (28cm) x 7" (18cm). Level the surface and bake at Gas Mark 4 or 180°C for about 35 minutes or until golden.

Allow to cool slightly, then cut into fingers.

Chicken in Apple and Onion Sauce

"Making exotic meals isn't just for the youngsters, you know – all my friends love this sweet and savoury dish when they visit for the evening."

Ingredients

12 oz (350g) cooked chicken, diced

1 medium green apple, peeled and diced

1 medium onion, peeled and chopped

2 sticks celery, chopped

4 fl oz (125ml) apple juice

3 oz (75g) butter or margarine

½ teaspoon (2.5ml) salt

¼ teaspoon (1.25ml) black pepper

a pinch of nutmeg

1 tablespoon (15ml) plain flour

¼ pint (150ml) double cream

Method

Melt three-quarters of the butter over a moderate heat. Add the apple, onion and celery and fry gently for 5 minutes. Add the apple juice, salt, pepper and nutmeg. Cover and simmer for 5 minutes. Remove lid and cook until most of the liquid has evaporated.

In a small saucepan, melt remaining butter, blend in the flour, then add the cream gradually. Add the sauce and chicken to the vegetables and heat through.

Serve with boiled rice, pasta or potatoes as preferred.

Lamb with French Beans

"If lamb's your favourite meat, why not try a change with this delicious recipe . . . (Lovely for Sunday lunch, but make sure that it's not mutton dressed as lamb!)"

Ingredients

1 lb (450g) boneless lamb cut in 1" (2.5cm) cubes

2 lb (900g) French beans, trimmed and cut into 2" (5cm) lengths

4 oz (110g) finely chopped onion

6 large tomatoes, peeled and chopped or 2 lb (900g) can tomatoes chopped and drained

1 teaspoon (5ml) salt

1 teaspoon (5ml) black pepper

½ teaspoon (2.5ml) nutmeg

½ teaspoon (2.5ml) allspice

2 ½ tablespoons (40ml) olive oil

Method

Spread beans evenly in bottom of large heavy casserole and set aside. Heat the oil over moderate heat, brown lamb deeply and evenly. Transfer to casserole.

Pour off oil except for a thin film. Cook the onions till soft, add to the lamb, then cover with tomatoes.

Add ¼ pint (150ml) water, sprinkle with seasonings and spices and cover. Place casserole over low heat, and simmer gently for about 1 hour. Serve with boiled rice.

Courgette and Tomato Bake

"My son's girlfriend doesn't eat meat, so when she comes for tea, I make her this tasty dish. It's a traditional way of cooking something new."

Ingredients

1 clove of garlic

2 large onions

4 tablespoons (60ml) cooking oil

1½ lb (700g) courgettes

8 oz (225g) tomatoes or 14 oz (400g) can of chopped tomatoes

1 tablespoon (15ml) chopped parsley

4 eggs

2 oz (50g) grated cheese

salt and pepper

a pinch of mixed herbs

Method

Skin and crush the garlic, peel and chop the onions. Heat the oil, and fry the garlic and onions for 3 - 4 minutes, until soft and rich coloured.

Wash and slice courgettes into ½" (10cm) slices. Add to the pan and fry for minutes, turning well. Skin and chop tomatoes (if fresh). Add to the pan with herbs and stir. Turn the mixture into a greased casserole dish.

Make 4 hollows with the back of a spoon, then break an egg into each. Sprinkle with grated cheese, and bake at Gas Mark 4 or 180°C for about 15 – 20 minutes until the eggs are set, and the cheese bubbles.

Tomato and Butter Bean Pie with Cheese Crust

"Don't be nervous about cooking for vegetarians – this recipe's easy to follow and you'll love the taste."

Ingredients

6 oz (175g) cheese pastry (see 'pastry' section in this book)

1 large can butter beans (or ½ lb (225g) dried beans)

1 large onion

½ teaspoonful (2.5ml) mixed herbs as liked

2 oz (50g) butter or margarine

1 tablespoon (15ml) tomato chutney

1 x 14oz (400g) can tomatoes

salt and pepper

Method

If using dried beans, soak them overnight and rinse, then cook until tender. If using canned beans, drain well.

Peel and chop the onion and fry with the herbs in the butter or margarine. Fry gently for 10 minutes. Add the beans, tomatoes and chutney.

Turn the mixture into a greased oven-proof dish, and top with pastry. Bake at Gas Mark 6 or 200°C for about 20 minutes. Serve with a green leaf vegetable.

Meat Balls in Tomato Sauce

"We had to be inventive cooks when I was a girl – and with limited resources too. The ingredients are easier to get now, but we always loved the Italian flavour, even then."

Ingredients

1lb (450g) minced beef
1 small onion, peeled and chopped
2 oz (50g) white breadcrumbs
½ teaspoon dried mixed herbs
a pinch of nutmeg
salt and pepper
1 egg, beaten
butter for frying

Sauce

1 large can tomatoes
1 small onion, peeled and chopped
2 oz (50g) mushrooms, chopped
1 stick celery, sliced thinly
2 teaspoons (10ml) tomato puree
1 teaspoon (5ml) sugar
½ teaspoon (2.5ml) dried mixed herbs
salt and pepper

Method

Mix all the ingredients for the meatballs together and bind with the egg. Use a little milk if not soft enough. Turn onto a floured board and divide into 16 pieces. Roll into balls and fry in butter, turning until lightly browned. Remove from the pan and fry the onions and celery until soft. Stir in the remaining ingredients and add meat balls.

Cover and simmer for about 30 minutes until the sauce thickens or meat balls are cooked. Serve with pasta and Parmesan cheese.

Potted Beef

"My grandmother taught me this one. When money was tight, it was a tasty and nourishing dish! Mmmm, lovely!"

Ingredients

1lb (450g) lean stewing beef

1 teaspoon (5ml) salt

6 tablespoons (90ml) water

a little butter

Method

Remove as much fat as possible from the beef and cut into small pieces. Put into a glass or stone jar.

Mix the salt well and add the water. Cover the jar with kitchen foil and stand it in a pan of hot water. Bring gently to the boil, then turn down the heat a little and boil for $2\frac{1}{2}$ hours, topping up the water when necessary.

Turn out the beef, season to taste and mince or pound up finely. Store in small pots, covering each with a thin layer of melted butter.

Floddies

"Floddies are not for people watching their weight – but they're definitely worth a try for a filling treat with a traditional breakfast . . . everyone will love them! Go on, forget the diet!"

Ingredients

2 large potatoes

1 tablespoon (15ml) flour

salt and pepper

fat for frying

Method

Peel the potatoes and grate them coarsely into a bowl. With the back of a tablespoon, press out as much water as possible. Season with salt and pepper, then mix in enough flour to bind.

Drop tablespoonfuls into the hot fat, flattening out like a pancake and fry on each side until golden brown.

Note: Grated cheese or finely chopped onion can be added to make either a tasty snack, or even a light meal if served with salad or green vegetables.

Bacon and Two-Bean Supper

"Want to warm the family on a winter's night? Then make this nutritious meal and you can't go wrong – you can be sure they'll be asking for more."

Ingredients

1 lb (450g) bacon or gammon pieces

1 lb (450g) new potatoes, scraped

4 oz (110g) broad beans, fresh or frozen

4 oz (110g) whole green beans, fresh or frozen

½ oz margarine

1 level tablespoon (15ml) flour

3 level tablespoons (45ml) chopped mint

¼ pint (150ml) water

salt and pepper

Method

Trim and de-rind the bacon, removing excess fat. Put into a frying pan, cover with water, bring to the boil, then discard the water and rinse the meat. Return to the pan. Add the potatoes, ¼ pint (150ml) water, mint and a sprinkle of pepper. Bring to simmering point – some froth may appear (this is salt in the meat) but will disappear as cooking continues. Cover the pan and simmer for 20 minutes.

Add the beans and cook for 5 minutes. Blend the margarine and flour to a paste. Dot in knobs over the beans and stir in. Bring to the boil and cook until the liquid thickens.

Simmer for 2 – 3 more minutes, or until vegetables are tender. Season to taste.

Minced Pork Pie

"A lovely little feast for Saturday lunch – and not hard on the pocket either! Don't buy 'em, bake 'em!"

Ingredients

1lb 2oz (500g) minced pork

1 large onion, peeled and finely chopped

½ teaspoon (2.5ml) salt

¼ teaspoon (1.25ml) black pepper

¼ teaspoon (1.25ml) dried marjoram

¼ teaspoon (1.25ml) dried thyme or sage

¼ pint (150ml) beef stock

2 tablespoons (30ml) plain flour

3 oz (75g) fine breadcrumbs

1 oz (25g) butter, cut into small pieces

Method

Heat the oven to Gas Mark 6 or 200°C.

In a medium sized frying pan, combine the pork, onion, salt, pepper and herbs. Add the stock and simmer for 10 minutes stirring occasionally. Tilt the pan, skim off any fat, then blend in the flour. Transfer to a greased 8" (200cm) pie dish.

Cover with breadcrumbs and dot with butter. Bake for about 15 minutes or until lightly browned. Serve with baked beans or red kidney beans.

Braised Brisket – Pot Roast

"The beauty of brisket is you get a tasty hot meal . . . and plenty of cold meat left over for sandwiches later. Brilliant brisket, I call it!"

Ingredients

2½ – 3 lbs (1.1kg – 1.4kg) rolled lean brisket

8 oz (225g) onions, peeled and quartered if large, or use baby onions

4 carrots, peeled and cut into thick strips

4 sticks celery, cut into 1½" (40cm) pieces

1 teaspoon (5ml) tarragon (or mixed herbs)

1 pint (570ml) beef stock (or water and stock cube)

1 tablespoon (15ml) corn or sunflower oil

Method

Heat the oil in a large heavy-based saucepan. Add the brisket and brown on all sides. Remove from the pan and add the vegetables and fry for 3 – 5 minutes. Return the meat to the pan, add the herbs and stock. Bring to the boil, then cover, reduce heat to low and cook for 40 minutes for each 1 lb (450g) of brisket weight.

Serve sliced with the vegetables and creamed potatoes.

Quick Gammon Casserole

"There's nothing I like better than getting down to some serious cooking – but when life gets too busy, I rely on this dish as a fast but satisfying meal. It's great!"

Ingredients

4 gammon steaks or chops

½ lb (225g) onions, peeled and sliced

1½ lb (700g) potatoes, peeled and sliced, thinly

½ lb (225g) frozen broad beans

1 tablespoon (15ml) oil

1 teaspoon (5ml) English mustard powder

1 ham or chicken stock cube – or stock

¼ pint (150ml) boiling water

pepper

Method

Heat the oil in a frying-pan and fry the steaks for 2 minutes each side, then spread with mustard. Dissolve the stock cube in the boiling water. Cover the gammon with the onions, then the beans and finally the potatoes, seasoning with pepper between each layer.

Pour over the stock, cover and simmer for 25 – 30 minutes, or until vegetables are cooked through.

Braised Liver Casserole

"I've never understood why some people don't like offal – it was a treat for me when I was a girl, I loved it! Especially in a casserole like this one – give it a go, it's really 'offally' nice!"

Ingredients

1 lb (450g) lamb's liver, sliced and floured (with about 1½ oz (40g) flour)

2 oz (50g) fat

3 medium onions, peeled and chopped

2 carrots, scraped and sliced

1 stick celery, sliced

4 bacon rashers, de-rinded and chopped

1 pint (570ml) of stock, or water and stock cube

Method

Pre-heat the oven to Gas Mark 4 or 180°C. Fry the liver, onions and bacon in the fat until sealed and lightly brown. Remove from the pan and fry the celery and carrot for about 3 minutes. Turn the mixture into a greased casserole dish, season and pour in the stock.

Cook in the centre of the oven for 45 minutes. Serve with creamed potatoes and a green vegetable.

Roast Stuffed Shoulder of Lamb

"Don't be nervous about serving up tried and tested traditional dishes – most people love meals like Mum used to make. And remember, sometimes the simplest is best!"

Ingredients

3½ – 4 lbs (1.6 – 1.8kg) rolled shoulder

1½ lbs (700g) potatoes

Stuffing

3 oz (75g) breadcrumbs

1 small onion, finely chopped

4 oz (110g) mushrooms, finely chopped

salt and pepper

1 egg

fat to roast

Method

Mix together the stuffing ingredients. Spread on the meat and roll or fold it into a neat shape. Secure with skewers, or tie with string. Melt the fat in the oven heated to Gas Mark 5 or 190°C.

Put the meat into the oven and baste. Par-boil the potatoes for 5 minutes, cut into halves, sprinkle with salt and cook for about 1½ hours, turning and basting from time to time.

Bacon and Egg Pie

"Brunch is a nice alternative for entertaining – pick a pie and prepare a positive feast!"

Ingredients

12 oz (350g) shortcrust pastry (see 'pastry' section in this book)

Filling

8 oz (225g) lean bacon rashers, thinly cut

4 large eggs

salt and pepper

Method

Roll out half of the pastry and use to line a greased 9" (23cm) pie plate. Lay half the bacon rashers on it. Break the eggs, leave them whole on top, and add the rest of the bacon. Season well with salt and pepper.

Roll out remaining dough and cover. Damp the edges to seal. Bake at Gas Mark 6 or 200°C for about 30 minutes, till pastry is golden.

West Country Casserole

"I'm borrowing this recipe from another region, and I discovered it one New Year when staying with friends in the West Country. It's a great idea for turkey leftovers and the cider gives it a proper tasty tang!"

Ingredients

1 lb (450g) turkey meat, cut into bite-size pieces

1 oz (25g) flour

1 level teaspoon (5ml) salt

¼ level teaspoon (1.25ml) mace

black pepper

8 oz (225g) onions, peeled and thinly sliced

1 dessert apple, cored and sliced

10 fl oz (275ml) dry cider

5 oz (150ml) soured cream

Method

Set the oven to Gas Mark 4 or 180°C. Mix the flour, salt, pepper and mace together and toss the turkey pieces to coat.

Heat 2 tablespoons (30ml) oil in a frying-pan and fry the turkey until lightly browned. Transfer to a greased casserole dish. Fry the onions for 2 minutes, then add to the meat. Add the cider and salt, carefully, to the pan, bring to the boil, then pour over the meat. Cook for 1 hour in the middle of the oven.

About 10 minutes before the end of the cooking time, add the sliced apple. Just before serving, stir in the soured cream.

Yorkshire Pudding

"Let's forget the War of the Roses while we're in the kitchen – after all, every good cook needs to know how to make Yorkshire Pudding!"

Ingredients

4 oz (110g) plain flour

½ teaspoon (2.5ml) salt

1 large egg

½ pint (275ml) of milk

2 tablespoons (30ml) cold water

fat

Method

Sieve flour and salt into a bowl. Break egg into the centre with a little milk. With a wooden spoon draw the flour from the sides and beat, adding milk gradually until a smooth batter is obtained. Leave to stand for 1 hour. Heat a little fat, into the dish to be used. Stir cold water into batter, and half fill the dish when fat is hot and smoking.

Bake at Gas Mark 7 or 220°C for about 20 minutes in hottest part of the oven. You can serve this with onion gravy, described on the next page.

Onion Gravy

Ingredients
(makes approx half pint (300 ml) gravy))
2 medium-sized onions (approx 7 oz (200g))
1 oz (25g) lard
1 oz (25g) plain flour

¾ pint (450ml) beef stock
pinch of grated nutmeg
1 teaspoon (5ml) wine vinegar
half teaspoon (2.5ml) made English or French mustard
salt and pepper

Method
Slice the onions. Melt the lard in a saucepan and fry the onion slowly until it is golden brown. Stir in the flour, reduce the heat and cook the flour very gently until it is also golden brown.

Draw pan off the heat and gradually add the stock, stirring all the time to prevent lumps forming.

Return to moderate heat and stir the sauce until boiling. Reduce the heat, cover and simmer for 30 minutes. Add a little grated nutmeg, the vinegar and mustard. Season to taste.

Serve with beef, offal or Yorkshire pudding.

PASTRY

This section describes how to make the four types of pastry used elsewhere in the book. See the 'healthy eating' section for hard fat substitutes.

Flaky Pastry

Ingredients

8 oz (225g) plain flour

6 oz (175g) margarine or margarine and butter mixed

½ teaspoon (2.5ml) salt

4 fl oz (125ml) cold water

1 teaspoon (5ml) lemon juice

Method

Sieve the flour and salt into a bowl. Divide the fat into 4 portions. Take one portion of fat and rub into the flour, lifting up hands to keep cool and airy until like breadcrumbs. Make a well in the centre, add lemon juice and enough cold water to make a firm (not sticky) dough, mixing it with a knife.

Turn onto a floured board and knead until smooth. Roll out into a strip three times as long as wide. Take a second portion of fat and dot it in even rows along the bottom of the strip, leaving half an inch (1cm) clear at the sides. Fold the top third of the strip over the bottom third, upwards and over. Turn the strip with its short edges to the top and bottom and roll out again as before. Repeat this process with the other portions of fat and leave it to rest for 15 minutes, then roll out.

Shortcrust Pastry

Ingredients

8 oz (225g) plain flour
4 oz margarine or hard fat
a pinch of salt
cold water to mix

Method

Sieve the flour and salt into a bowl. Rub the fat into the flour and salt to breadcrumb stage (i.e. until the mixture resembles breadcrumbs). Add water and mix to a soft, not sticky dough. Roll out to use.

Cheese Pastry

Ingredients

6 oz (175g) self raising flour
3 oz (75g) margarine or hard fat
4 oz (110g) grated cheese
a pinch of salt
cold water to mix

Method

Sieve the flour and salt into a bowl. Rub in the fat to bread-crumb stage (i.e. when the mixture starts to resemble bread-crumbs). Add the grated cheese and mix with water to a soft (not sticky) dough. Roll out to use.

Rough Puff Pastry

Ingredients

8oz (225g) plain flour
½ teaspoon (2.5ml) salt
6 oz (175ml) margarine and lard mixed
cold water to mix

Method

Mix the flour and salt. Cut the fat into small pieces about the size of a hazelnut. Stir in using a fork and adding enough cold water to make a stiff paste.

On a floured board, roll into a long strip. Turn the top third towards you. Turn the bottom third over and seal the edges with a rolling pin. Then, turn the sealed edge towards you.

Roll out again, turning as before and repeat once again – 3 rollings in all. Leave to stand for 15 minutes before using.

CAKES & PUDDINGS

This is a small selection of traditional cakes and puddings to complement Mildred's Main Meals. See the 'healthy eating' section for hard fat substitutes.

Country Apple Cake

"I used to go apple-picking with my brothers in the orchard down the lane – and if we didn't get caught, Mum would make them into a tasty Country Apple Cake for tea. Here's how you do it."

Ingredients

8 oz (225g) self-raising flour

a pinch of salt

4 oz (110g) butter or margarine

4 oz (110g) granulated sugar

1 lb (450g) cooking apples

1 egg, beaten

2 – 3 tablespoons (30 – 45ml) milk

Method

Pre-heat the oven to Gas Mark 4, 350°F or 180°C. Grease a small roasting tin (or dish) approximately 8" x 10" (20cm x 25cm). Sift flour and sugar into a large mixing bowl, rub in the fat until the mixture looks like breadcrumbs.

Peel and core the apples, chop into small pieces and mix into the flour. Add the beaten egg, and just enough milk to make a very stiff dough. Turn the mixture into roasting tin, sprinkle with sugar, and bake for 30 – 35 minutes, until golden.

Serve hot with cream or custard, or cold, cut into slices.

Parkin

"I'm in trouble if I don't make a tray of Parkin when the family comes to visit – it's not just a bonfire feast, you know, it's fine for any winter's night!"

Ingredients

4 oz (110g) plain flour
8 oz (225g) medium oatmeal
8 oz (225g) soft brown sugar
8 oz (225g) black treacle
2 oz (50g) butter
1 oz (25g) lard
1 egg, beaten
2 level teaspoons (10ml) ground ginger
½ level teaspoon (2.5ml) ground cinnamon
¼ level teaspoon (1.25ml) bicarbonate of soda
5 – 6 tablespoons (75 – 90ml) milk

Method

Set the oven to Gas Mark 3 or 160°C. Sift the flour, spices and soda into a bowl, stir in the oatmeal. Gently heat the butter, lard, treacle and sugar in a large saucepan. Stir the melted mixture into the dry ingredients, add the egg and milk and beat until smooth.

Pour into a deep 7" (18cm) tin, greased and with the base lined. Bake in the middle of the oven for 1½ hours, or until firm to the touch. When cold, wrap in foil and keep for a week before eating.

Note: Parkin often sinks in the middle when baking. This is usual – don't worry!

John Peel Tart

"I always like a dish with a tale to tell — this recipe came from a farmer's wife in the Lakes, from the story of that famous Cumbrian huntsman. Perhaps you know the song . . . ?"

Ingredients

8 oz shortcrust pastry (see 'pastry' section in this book) to line a
    7" (18cm) or 8" (20cm) plate.

Filling

6 oz (175g) currants

4 oz (110g) ground almonds

2 oz (50g) butter

2 oz (50g) sugar

½ teaspoon (2.5ml) mixed spice

2 teaspoons (10ml) lemon juice

Method

Warm the butter and sugar, combine with other ingredients
and spread over pastry. Top with extra pastry, lattice if preferred. Bake at Gas Mark 6 or 200°C for 40 minutes. This can
be eaten hot or cold, with cream.

Bakewell Pudding

"Have you ever been to the beautiful little town of Bakewell? It's in Derbyshire and it's well worth a visit – and it is, of course, the inspiration for this pudding (not 'tart', please note, but 'pudding'). Go on, give it a whirl!"

Ingredients

8 oz (225g) flaky pastry (see 'pastry' section in this book)

Filling

2 heaped tablespoons (30ml) of jam (strawberry or apricot)

3 eggs

3 oz (75g) caster sugar

3 oz (75g) ground almonds

4 oz (110g) melted butter

Method

Roll out the flaky pastry to line an 8" (20cm) pie plate or dish – preferably 2" (5cm) or 3" (8cm) deep. Warm jam and spread evenly over base. Beat eggs and sugar until creamy, stir in almonds and melted butter and pour over jam.

Bake in the centre of the oven at Gas Mark 6 or 200°C for about 25 – 30 minutes, until filling is set. Serve hot with cream.

Bread and Butter Pudding

"Here's one the kids will always choose over ready-made puddings – let's show 'em how good it was when we were young."

Ingredients

4 slices brown bread, crusts removed

marmalade

butter

1 pint (570ml) of milk

2 eggs

1 oz (25g) sugar

 nutmeg or cinnamon as preferred

Method

Spread the bread with butter and marmalade and cut each piece into four triangles. Layer in a greased pudding dish. Beat the eggs into the milk and pour over the bread. Leave to stand for 1 hour.

Sprinkle the sugar and spice over the top before baking. Bake at Gas Mark 4 or 180°C for about 35 minute or until set.

Note: this is a variation on the usual recipe, which uses white bread and about 3 oz (75g) of dried fruit.

Brandy Snaps

"My lot always opt for the whipped cream – what a treat at a party . . . or even just for tea!"

Ingredients

2 oz (50g) plain flour

3 oz (75g) butter

2 oz (50g) caster sugar

3 oz (75g) golden syrup

1 teaspoon (5ml) ground ginger

whipped cream

Method

Melt the sugar, syrup and fat in a pan, cool slightly, then stir in the flour and ginger. Mix well, then place teaspoonsfuls of the mixture, well apart, on greased silicone paper.

Bake at Gas Mark 4 or 180°C for 10 – 15 minutes. Remove with a palette knife when they are just beginning to get crisp and roll up. This is easier to do around the greased handle of a wooden spoon. When cold, fill with whipped cream.

Alternative Recipe

Ingredients

2 oz (50g) plain flour

2 oz (50g) butter

4 oz (100g) caster sugar

2 oz (50g) syrup

1 teaspoon (5ml) ground ginger

a pinch of mixed spice

Method

As above. Bake at Gas Mark 6 or 200°C.

Cup of Tea Loaf

"When you're having a cosy winter afternoon around the fire, what's nicer than a piece of wholesome Cup of Tea Loaf? It's always a warming winner in my house!"

Ingredients

8 oz (225g) self raising flour

3 oz (75g) butter or margarine

3 oz (75g) granulated sugar

4 oz (110g) mixed dried fruit

1 tablespoon (15ml) marmalade

1 teaspoon (5ml) bicarbonate of soda

¼ pint (150ml) cold strained tea (strong)

Methods

Bring the tea and the fruit to the boil, simmer for 5 minutes, then add the bicarbonate of soda and allow to cool. Mix the butter or margarine and sugar together, add the flour and cool liquid, lastly the marmalade and mix well. Turn mixture into a greased loaf tin, and bake at Gas Mark 4 or 180°C for 1 hour.

Leave for 24 hours before eating. To serve, dredge with caster sugar, then slice and butter.

Irish Soda Bread

"A good friend of mine from Ireland taught me about this bread – it's always been a hit with my family and it's surprisingly quick and easy to make."

Ingredients

8 oz (225g) wholemeal self-raising flour

4 oz (110g) white self-raising flour

1 level teaspoon (5ml) bicarbonate of soda

1 level teaspoon (5ml) salt

approx. ½ pint (275ml) of sour milk or buttermilk

(If neither is available, add a tablespoon (15ml) of lemon juice or vinegar to ordinary milk)

Method

Mix flours, add bicarbonate of soda and salt to milk, and mix well. Turn the dough onto a floured board, knead till smooth, and form into a round of about 7" (180cm). Cut a cross across the middle, so it bakes into a quartered shape.

Turn into a greased cake tin and bake for 40 – 45 minutes in the centre of the oven at Gas Mark 5 or 190°C.

Index

More books from Sigma Leisure

We publish a wide range of books for North-West England
and further afield. Here is a small selection:

Seashore Sea Food: How to Catch it, Cook it and Prepare it!	£4.95
Liverpool Alehouses: including the Wirral	£6.95
Traditional Pubs of Old Lancashire	£7.95
Golf Courses of Cheshire	£9.95
50 Best Cycle Rides in Cheshire	£7.95
Cycling in The Lake District	£7.95
100 Lake District Hill Walks	£7.95
Lakeland Walking: On The Level	£6.95
Teashop Walks in The Lake District	£6.95
Lakeland Rocky Rambles	£9.95
Mostly Downhill (series of 3 books covering the Lake District, Dark Peak and White Peak)	£6.95 each
Rambles around Manchester	£5.95
Best Pub Walks in & around Manchester	£6.95
Best Pub Walks around Chester & The Dee Valley	£6.95
Pub Walks in Lancashire	£6.95
Pub Walks in the Lake District	£6.95
Portrait of Manchester	£6.95
Ghosts, Traditions amd Legends of Old Lancashire	£7.95
Great Days Out! Manchester area	£4.95

All of our books are available from your bookseller. In case
of difficulty, or for our complete catalogue, please contact:

Sigma Leisure, 1 South Oak Lane, Wilmslow, Cheshire
SK9 6AR. Tel: 01625-531035; Fax: 01625-536800

Cheques payable to SIGMA PRESS.
Major credit cards welcome